# RYA Start \

Edited by Amanda Van Santen

© RYA 2006

First Published 2006

**The Royal Yachting Association**

RYA House, Ensign Way, Hamble

Southampton SO31 4YA

**Tel**: 0845 345 0400

**Fax**: 0845 345 0329

**Email**: publications@rya.org.uk

**Web**: www.rya.org.uk

**ISBN**: 1905104359

**RYA Order Code**: G49

Totally Chlorine Free

Sustainable Forests

A CIP record of this book is available from the British Library

**Note:** While all reasonable care has been taken in the preparation of this book, the publisher takes no responsibility for the use of the methods or products or contracts described in the book.

Telephone 0845 345 0400 for a free copy of our Publications Catalogue.

**Cover Design**: Pete Galvin
**Photographs**: Peter Van Santen
**Illustrations**: Pete Galvin
**Typeset**: Creativebyte
**Proofreading and indexing**: Alan Thatcher
**Printed in China through**: World Print
**Acknowlegments**: Minorca Sailing Holidays, Chichester Watersports Centre, Simon Winkley, Gul, Mark Warner

# Contents

| Chapter | | Page |
|---|---|---|

# CHAPTER 2

# RYA National Windsurfing Scheme

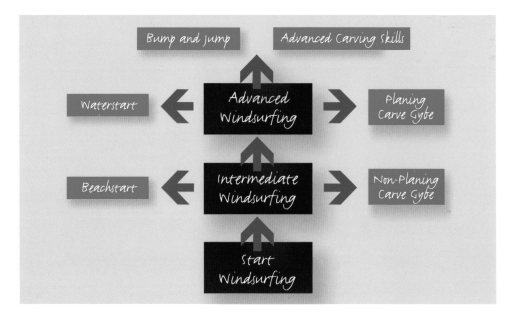

## Start Windsurfing
An introduction to the sport teaching you the basics to get you up and sailing around in as little as 8 hours.

## Intermediate Windsurfing
Learn and make use of the unique Fast*fwd* coaching formula in order to get to grips with the harness, footstraps and the more dynamic skills in stronger winds. This section is divided into non-planing and planing levels of achievement.

## Additional Intermediate Clinics
Beachstarting and gybing are taught either as a clinic or combined in a RYA course tailored to the needs of the individual in their particular learning environment.

## Advanced Windsurfing
Improve your blasting control and confidence while tacking. The Fast*fwd* coaching formula is used to break down and simplify each skill. Lower volume boards are used in a variety of conditions.

## Additional Advanced Clinics
Learn how to use your gybing skills to master the carve gybe to get around the corners fast. Use your beachstart skills to tackle the waterstart. Further add to your repertoire with carve variations in the advanced carving skills clinic and basic jumping in the bump and jump clinic.

# CHAPTER 3

# RYA Start Windsurfing Course

The National Windsurfing Scheme takes you progressively through the skills required to become a competent windsurfer in a variety of conditions. Each level enables you to log your progression, set goals and enhance your knowledge and understanding of both the environment you windsurf in and the mechanics of the sport. In addition to the practical elements, each section covers a small amount of windsurfing background knowledge.

**Start Windsurfing**
An introduction to the sport teaching you the fundamentals to get you up and sailing around in as little as 8 hours. There are no prerequisites to this course other than a degree of water confidence.

Upon completing the course, the instructor will log your progression in the 'RYA National Windsurfing Logbook and Syllabus (G47)'. The centre principal or chief instructor will decide whether a certificate is to be awarded or advise you that further practice is required providing you with a clear pathway to gain your certificate.

# CHAPTER 4

# Equipment

Although at first glance it may seem that you need a lot of equipment to go windsurfing, in reality there are just three essentials to think about: the board, the rig and you!

This section will briefly take you through the most important aspects of each of these three essentials helping you to quickly learn the names of the equipment you will use and how to look after yourself and your kit.

## The Board

### Size
An ideal beginners' board should be wide for stability, durable and buoyant.

### Front and back
The **'nose'**, or 'front end', is slightly more pointed and curving upwards giving a smoother ride. The **'tail'**, or 'back of the board', is squarer or more rounded in shape and without an upward curve.

### Top and bottom
The **'deck'**, or 'top of the board', usually has a rough feel and is covered by a non-slip surface. The **'hull'**, or 'bottom of the board', is smooth producing little resistance when travelling through the water.

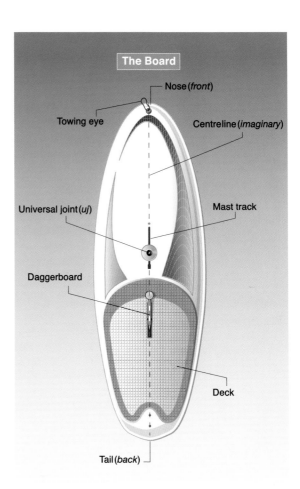

The Board

Nose *(front)*

Towing eye

Centreline *(imaginary)*

Universal joint *(uj)*

Mast track

Daggerboard

Deck

Tail *(back)*

## Daggerboard

A large, flat plate which slides vertically through the middle of the board. It is fully retractable allowing you to sail in shallow waters. The **daggerboard** provides some resistance and when in the down position, stops the board from going sideways and gives a little more stability. When learning to windsurf it should be in the 'down' position all the time. Some boards have a smaller, fixed, semi-circular centre 'fin'.

## Fin

Shaped like a dorsal fin, a smaller flat plate attached to the underside and tail end of the board. Its role is to give directional stability (it helps with steering and controls the direction of the board).

## Mast track

The recess on the top of the board, (just in front of the daggerboard slot), into which the **mastfoot** and **universal joint** is attached (the base of the rig - see 'The Rig' on page 8).

## Centreline

An imaginary line running down the middle of the board from nose to tail, important in aiding stability when you are standing on the board.

## Towing eye

A small hole in the nose of the board through which a rope can be passed for towing. Some boards have larger holes that double up as a carrying aid.

---

**Top tip**

The buoyancy (or volume) of boards is measured in litres. 1 litre will support 1 kg. An 80 kg adult learning to windsurf should be using a board with at least 200 litres of volume to ensure good buoyancy.

Calculation:

   80kg (person)
+ 20kg (the rig's weight)
x 2
   200 = litres for a stable beginner's board

---

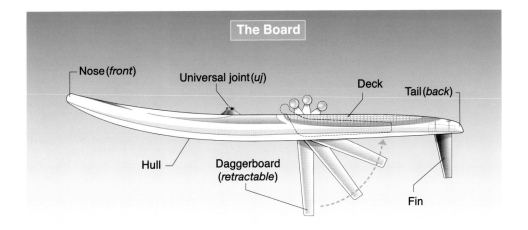

The Board

Nose *(front)* — Universal joint *(uj)* — Deck — Tail *(back)*

Hull — Daggerboard *(retractable)* — Fin

# The Rig

## Mast

Long, tapered pole (thicker at the bottom, thinner at the top) which holds the sail up. Available in different heights, diameters, weights and materials. The mast should, above all, be suitable for the sail.

## Sail

The 'engine' of a windsurfer, made from strengthened, almost triangular-shaped material working with the wind to deliver power to the windsurfer. Available in different sizes, weights and materials it is crucial that the sail is light enough and of a suitable size to handle easily. Other parts that together make up the sail are: the luff tube, head, leech, clew, foot and tack.

## Battens

Stiff, flexible rods fitted in some sails which provide extra power, stability and shape.

## Boom

Effectively the handlebars of the windsurfer, the bar you hold onto when sailing and the tool to control the rig. Very easy to attach to the mast and sail.

## Mastfoot

An attachment which joins the rig, via the bottom of the mast, to the board. There are many different designs and types but it is important that the mastfoot is kept in good condition.

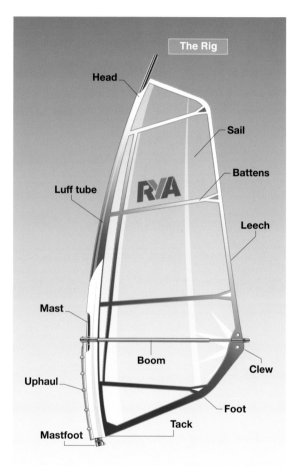

## Uphaul

Probably the single most important piece of equipment while learning to windsurf! The uphaul is a piece of combined rope and elastic which, once attached to the front of the boom and mastfoot, can be used to lift the rig out of the water.

# Personal Equipment

## Wetsuits

Usually made from neoprene and available in different thicknesses, styles and colours. Designed to provide some insulation to the body by trapping a thin layer of water between the body and the suit which is warmed up by body heat. The most common types available are:

- Winter suit or steamer: A full body suit that is suitable for cold conditions, usually 5mm in thickness.

- Autumn/spring or convertible suit: A suit with short arms and long legs. Sometimes with detachable long arm pieces, and 3mm in thickness.

- Summer or shortie suit: Has short arms and legs and is designed for hot or tropical conditions, and 2mm in thickness.

When buying a suit make sure it is suitable for the weather conditions you will be sailing in, that it fits well, is comfortable when bending and that the neck allows you enough freedom of movement so you can easily look around. Manufacturers do make suits specifically designed for windsports.

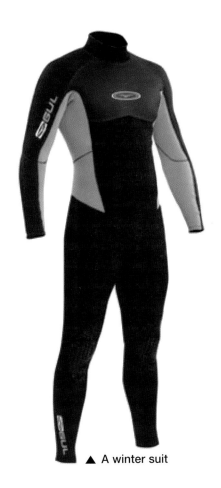

▲ A winter suit

Wetsuit boots ▶

## Footwear

Shoes known as booties or boots, though not essential, are a good idea to wear while windsurfing. Made from a combination of neoprene and rubber and of different thicknesses, they provide some insulation, grip and protection from bumps and scrapes. Make sure they are a good fit and designed especially for windsurfing or surfing with a thin bendy sole and a good grip.

## Buoyancy aids

When learning to windsurf it is important to wear a buoyancy aid. A buoyancy aid is designed to help a conscious person stay afloat in the water. A buoyancy aid should be the correct size, fit well and not slip up or over your head when you are in the water.

## ▼ Keep yourself warm and protected

### Rash vests

Worn under a wetsuit and originally designed by surfers to prevent getting a rash on their chests when paddling, rash vests, or 'rashies', are thin tops with short or long sleeves.

Thermal rash vests are available - rash vests with a thin insulating layer of neoprene - which offer a bit of insulation but not as much as a wetsuit. UV protection rash vests are now available for those hot summer days when you do not need to wear a wetsuit. As with wetsuits, the fit of a rash vest must be good.

### Gloves

Available in long or short-fingered in a variety of thickness and materials, worn for warmth or to protect the fingers and hands.

### Hats

Again an optional extra, neoprene hats (for those extremely cold days) and helmets which offer extra protection and widely used. Make sure the fit is good, that it is designed for windsurfing and is not heavy and cumbersome.

# CHAPTER 5

# Rigging

Knowing how to rig a sail is a great way to becoming more involved and independent and may eventually lead to you buying and owning your own rig. Practise how to rig as many designs and models as possible to build your confidence.

A simple, step-by-step approach to rigging:

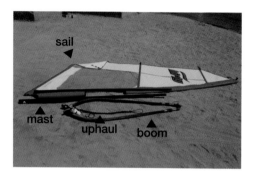

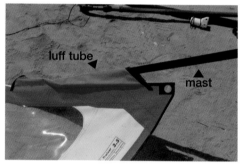

1. Lay all the components of the **rig** out on the ground.

2. Slide the **mast** up the **luff tube** (thin end first) to the head of the **sail** or head cap.

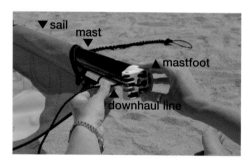

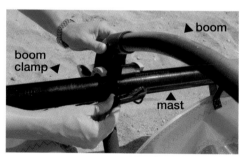

3. Put the **mastfoot** into the base of the mast and thread the **downhaul** line through the eyelet or pulley system at the bottom of the sail, applying a small amount of tension.

4. Attach the front of the **boom** to the **mast** using the **boom clamp** and take care to make sure it is tight, and won't slip. Do not worry too much about boom height as this can be adjusted later.

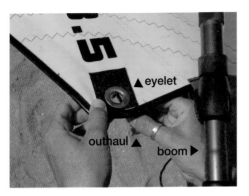

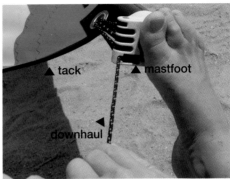

5. Thread the **outhaul** through the cleats on the end of the **boom** and through the **eyelet** on the **sail**, applying a small amount of tension.

6. Pull on the **downhaul** until the **tack** is down to the **mastfoot**. This may sometimes require some effort!

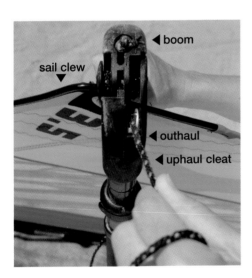

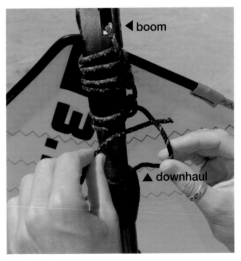

7. Pull on the **outhaul** until the **clew** is next to the end of the **boom**. This will require less effort than applying the **downhaul tension**!

8. Remember to tie off any loose ropes and check that the **uphaul** is attached to the **mastfoot** and the front end of the **boom**.

**9.** To finish off, stand the rig upright and adjust the **boom height** so that it is between chest and shoulder height.

To de-rig, carry out the above process in reverse, taking care to release the tension from the downhaul and outhaul gently and gradually.

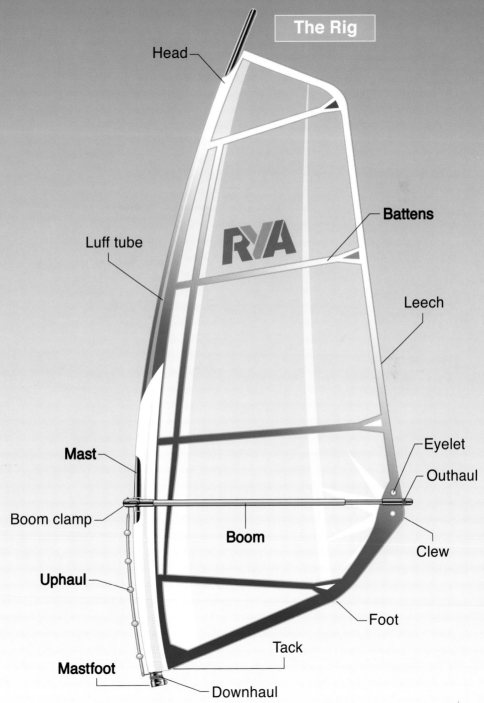

The Rig

Head

Battens

Luff tube

Leech

RYA

Mast

Eyelet

Boom clamp

Outhaul

Boom

Clew

Uphaul

Foot

Tack

Mastfoot

Downhaul

# CHAPTER 6

# Wind Awareness

Up to now the wind may have been nothing more to you than a nuisance; blowing your hair around, slamming a door or window or blowing litter down the street. Once you start windsurfing it becomes increasingly important. As the name 'windsurfing' suggests, wind is the most necessary ingredient for the sport!

It is essential that you have an understanding and awareness of where the wind is coming from and fortunately there are many ways of establishing this.

- Flags are one of the easiest indicators - they flutter in the direction the wind is blowing and are, luckily for us, everywhere in RYA Windsurfing centres.
- The wind you feel on your face when out on the water is a great indicator, especially if you can't see any flags on the beach!
- Ripples on the water usually move in the direction the wind is blowing from, clearly showing the wind direction.

Once you can work out where the wind is coming from, there are a few terms that will be helpful to you:

- If something is referred to as **downwind** then it means it is closer to where the wind is blowing **to**.
- If something is **upwind** then it is closer to where the wind is blowing **from**.
- If something is referred to as **across the wind** it means that it is at <u>90° to the wind</u>.

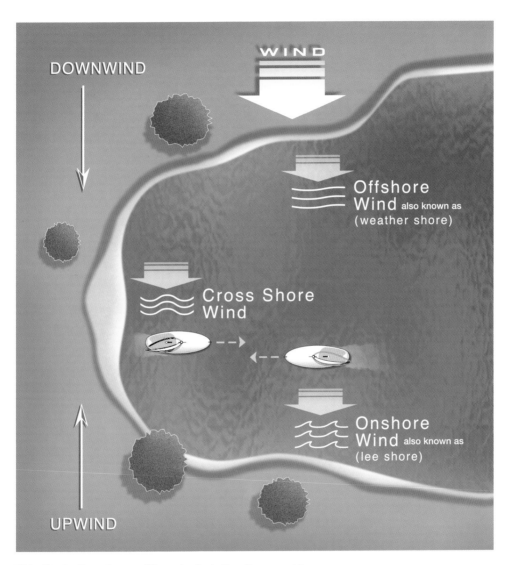

This illustration shows different wind directions and terms.

# CHAPTER 7

# Carrying and Launching

Now that you are primed and ready to get out on the water it is necessary to quickly look at how to carry the kit to and from the water. To begin it is easier to carry each item separately, because the combination of board and rig is quite heavy to lift and carry on land.

There is no set order in which the kit should be taken down to or brought back from the water but there are some important safety points to bear in mind.

**1. Leaving kit safely on the shore**
When leaving kit unattended on land always attach the rig to the board, with the board at 90° to the wind and the mast pointing to where the wind is blowing to.

**2. The rig**
The art of carrying the rig lies in allowing the wind to blow under the sail so that it does all the lifting for you. Stand upwind of the rig with the mast at 90° to the wind, and the rest of the rig downwind, grab the upper side of the boom with one hand and the mast with the other. Lift the rig and walk with your back to the wind towards the water.

If you take the rig down to the water before the board, remember the rig is very light and is likely to fly away if left unattended. You can, for the few moments it takes to go and get the board, place the rig in the water. This is also a good method when landing so that the board can be taken up the beach first.

If the board is taken down to the water first and the rig left alone on the land it must be attached or weighted down at or around the mastfoot to something solid with the mast pointing downwind, or it may blow away!

## 3. The board

The board is made of a tough substance (such as plastic) which, although durable, does weigh more than the rig. Try to get someone to help you carry the board each holding an end.

When carrying the board on your own, roll the board onto its side and, standing on the same side as the hull (bottom of the board), reach over and grab the daggerboard handle or, if fitted, the carry-aid. Lift by using your legs and not your back.

Alternatively, with the board on its side, stand on the same side as the deck (top of the board) and, with the daggerboard in the 'down' position, reach over and grab the blade of the daggerboard and lift, again using your legs, not your back! This method also works for boards with centre fins.

Once board and rig are in the water, attach them together and you're ready to go!

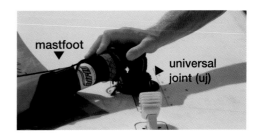

# CHAPTER 8

# The Secure Position

The **secure position** is a neutral or 'safe' position that can be adopted when standing on the board having lifted the rig out of the water.

From the secure position it is possible to position the board where you want it, turn it around and generally get settled. It is a good idea to always get into the secure position before sailing off, slowing down or stopping.

Simple, step-by-step approach to getting into the secure position:

1. Walk the board and rig out into waist / thigh-deep water. Put the daggerboard down and line the board across the wind, with the rig lying on the downwind side (the side furthest away from the wind).

2. Approach the board from the opposite side to the rig, place your hands over the centreline (the imaginary line running down the middle of the board) and pull your body over the board.

3. Bring your knees onto the board, keeping your weight over the centreline. Grasp the uphaul rope for stability and check that the wind is still coming from behind you.

4. Get onto your feet, placing them either side of the mastfoot and over the centreline. With bent knees, leaning back slightly and holding the uphaul rope with straight arms, stand up - using your legs and not your back - and pull the rig partially clear of the water.

5. Work hand-over-hand up the uphaul to pull the rig out of the water completely. Grasping the mast with both hands below the boom, keeping your arms extended.

6. Get into a comfortable, relaxed position with arms extended, knees slightly bent and with your head up, with a V-shape forming between your body and the rig.

To check your position across the wind:

**7.** Lean the rig towards the back of the board and the front will turn towards the wind.

**8.** Lean the rig towards the front of the board and the front will turn away from the wind.

**9.** You have now completed the secure position!

**Top tips for the secure position**

- Keep your weight over the centreline of the board.

- Use your legs, not your back, to pull the rig out of the water.

- Maintain a comfortable, relaxed position, arms extended, knees slightly bent and head up, with a V-shape formed between your body and the rig.

## Upwind Rig Recovery

There are times when you are about to get onto your board and you notice that the rig is lying upwind of the board. Instead of tiring yourself out by swimming the rig downwind of the board, or getting frustrated by uphauling into the secure position only to get thrown off by the rig as it makes its way downwind, try this simple method:

1. Get onto the board from the opposite side to the rig, this time you will be facing the wind as opposed to having it on your back.

2. Lift the rig partially out of the water (remember to use legs) and wait for the wind to catch the sail, which will then gently swing the board around.

3. Once you have your back to the wind you can then resume uphauling into the secure position.

# CHAPTER 9

# Static turning (and taking the board 180º)

Once up on the board and holding the rig in the secure position, you are controlling the board and rig in readiness to start sailing, this position can be developed to assist in turning the board.

Practising turning or static steering of the board while stationary helps develop a good understanding of steering the board when sailing and is a very useful way to spin the board around a 180º turn in a tight space.

As shown in the previous chapter 'Secure Position' (page 20), when leaning the rig to the back of the board the front will turn towards the wind. Leaning the rig forwards will turn the board away.

To develop this skill further here are some easy-to-follow steps for turning the board effectively through 180º while stationary:

**1.** Starting from the secure position, lean the rig to the back of the board.

**2.** As you steer, the front of the board will turn towards the wind.

**3.** Take small steps around the mastfoot - on the opposite side to the direction the rig is moving.

**4.** Keeping the rig inclined and moving across the board (either to the front or the back), remembering to keep your arms extended.

The board can also be turned away from the wind by leaning the rig to the front of the board and taking steps around the mastfoot.

**5.** Return to the secure position once the board has turned through 180°.

**Top tips for static turning**

- Always keep your arms extended when leaning the rig to the back (or front) of the board.
- The further you lean the rig towards either end of the board, the faster the board will turn.
- Take small steps when moving your feet around the mastfoot.
- Ensure that you return to the secure position once you have turned the board through 180°.

# CHAPTER 10

# The Sailing Position

Once you are standing on the board at 90° to the wind in your secure position, you are ready to start sailing.

Steps to get you going:

1. From the secure position pick out somewhere to aim for - a **goal point** across the wind and in the direction the board is facing (a house on the land is good).

2. Take your front hand off the mast and move it across onto the boom, once comfortable take your back hand off the mast as well.

**3.** Gently move your back foot behind the daggerboard, keeping it across the centreline, also bringing your front foot back slightly so that it is next to the mastfoot, facing forwards.

4. Turn your shoulders to face your goal point, at the same time pulling the rig across you to where it feels light and balanced - this is called the **'balance point'**.

5. Immediately place your back hand on the boom and pull the sail in gently, counter balancing the weight and movement of the rig by bending your back leg slightly and dropping your body back and down, (remembering to keep looking where you are going).

**6.** Finally, reposition your feet, hands and body until you feel comfortable.

**You are now sailing across the wind.**

**To stop or slow down:**

**1.** If you want to slow down or come to a controlled stop, release your back hand from the boom and return to the secure position.

**2.** If you need to stop quickly, repeat the above process but lower the rig into the water to put the brakes on, crouching down quickly on the board.

---

**Top tips for sailing across the wind**

- Always select a goal point across the wind and keep looking at it while sailing.
- Remember to always draw the rig across you to its **balance point** before pulling in on the boom with your back hand.
- At all times use your body to counterbalance the movement and weight of the rig.
- Try to keep your movement smooth and flowing at all times.

# CHAPTER 11

# Steering and Tacking the Board

Now that you are up and windsurfing it is a good idea to practise how to steer your board to enable you to control the direction the board is travelling, helping to avoid running into other people or objects out on the water. This is also a good opportunity to learn how to turn the board around in a more stylish and controlled manner rather than just pivoting it 180° as you learnt earlier (page 24).

## Steering

Steering the board while sailing uses the same principles as manoeuvring the board during 'static turning' (page 24). This section takes you through the technique of how to steer your board while on the move.

**To steer towards the wind:**

1. While windsurfing across the wind, look upwind and select a new object or goal point to aim for.

2. Draw the rig across your body and towards the back of the board, extending your back arm. The board will steer towards the wind.

**3.** When heading towards your new upwind goal point, bring the rig back to the normal sailing position and pull it in slightly with your back hand.

**To steer away from the wind:**

**4.** From your new 'upwind' sailing position, look downwind towards your original across-wind goal point. Draw the rig across your body and towards the front of the board, extending your front arm and pulling in with your back arm. As the rig moves in front of you, drop your body back and keep it low to counter balance the movement of the rig. The board will then steer away from the wind.

**5.** When you are heading back towards your original across-wind goal point, bring the rig back to the normal sailing position and ease out slightly with your back arm.

**Top tips for steering**

- Always look towards where you want to steer - your goal point - and keep looking at it.
- Remember to always counterbalance any movement of the rig with your body.

## Turning the Board

The 'static turning' section (page 24) explained how to manoeuvre and turn your board through 180°. This next section will look at how to turn the board around in a controlled and fluid manner and with the nose of the board moving through the 'eye' of the wind. This type of turn is called a **'tack'**.

Step-by-step approach to tacking: From a sailing position across the wind, steer the board upwind as you did in **'steering'** (page 30).

1. From a sailing position closer to the wind, look upwind and moving your front hand off the boom placing it on the mast (just below the boom) and placing your front foot in front of the mastfoot, extending your back arm. As the rig moves back, remember to counterbalance with your body. The board will steer into the wind and start to slow down.

2. Bring your back foot up to join your front foot in front of the mast and move your back hand off the boom and place it on the mast.

**3.** Keeping the rig inclined, continue to move it over the back of the board, taking small steps with your feet around the mastfoot on to the opposite side of the board.

**4.** Continue doing this until you are back in the secure position and with the nose of the board facing 180° in the opposite direction from where you started.

**5.** Return to your sailing position, heading in the opposite direction across the wind.

**Top tips for tacking**

- Always look where you want to go when steering the board into the wind.

- Throughout the turn remember to always use your body to counterbalance the movement and weight of the rig.

- Always return to the secure position at the end of a tack enabling you to gain your bearings before setting off again.

# CHAPTER 12

# Stance

Stance is a broad term that describes a windsurfer's position when standing on the board holding the rig. A good stance should feel comfortable and suit the conditions you are sailing in. Divided into four aspects: head, arms, legs and body, the same basic principles are used by all windsurfers whether they are beginning the sport or an accomplished professional blasting around at high speeds, doing the latest freestyle tricks or pulling off impressive aerial acrobatics in waves. The key is to have the fundamentals correct from the start which will allow you to work at developing more advanced skills.

### Head
Your head should always be turned to look where you want to go, this enables you to be aware of your surroundings and avoid running into things!

### Arms
Your arms should be extended so that the rig is at a comfortable distance from your body. Keep your hands shoulder-width apart on the boom and in a position where you can feel equal pressure on both arms (usually one-third of the way down the boom from the mast).

### Legs
Your legs should be relatively straight but ready to flex (rather like shock absorbers) with your feet comfortably shoulder-width apart and positioned so that the board is flat and stable. Generally your front foot should be facing forwards with your back foot across the board.

### Body
When windsurfing it is necessary to keep changing your body position in order to keep feeling stable and comfortable. Generally, by concentrating on your head, arms and legs you will end up in a good position.

However, if you do not feel in control, for example because you are in stronger winds, choppier water, or going slightly faster with a bigger sail, then you should adopt a lower body position by dropping your hips over a flexed back leg.

Alternatively, if you feel slightly inefficient and sluggish in your windsurfing, perhaps because there are very light winds or you are using a very small sail, straighten your body position by lifting your hips and allowing your back leg to straighten.

The photo above illustrates a good windsurfing stance when windsurfing across the wind. Note how the four basic principles of head, arms, legs and body are being followed to achieve an effective stance for all conditions.

# CHAPTER 13

# Safety and Self-Rescue

As with any sport as a beginner you should ensure that you know how to look after yourself enabling you to relax and enjoy the experience.

Generally, windsurfing is very safe, especially if you are learning at an RYA Centre where there are qualified instructors and safety boats on a carefully chosen safe stretch of water. Nevertheless, you should be aware of the fundamentals of how to help yourself both on and off the water should any problems arise. This knowledge will also increase your confidence and help with your development in the sport.

## Prevention Rather than Cure

In windsurfing, as in any situation, it is always better to prevent a problem arising rather than stumbling into it and then trying to fix it. There are some easy-to-remember gems of information that help you to be prepared and safe before, during and after you head out on the water. These are known as the **'seven common senses'**:

1. **Is all your equipment seaworthy and suitable?**

   **Clothing**
   Make sure you are wearing suitable clothing to keep warm and comfortable during your windsurfing session. At a minimum: wetsuit, boots and a buoyancy aid should be worn.

   **The Board**
   Check the mastfoot for signs of wear. The rubber or hinged part of the mastfoot should have a built-in safety strap to keep the rig attached to the board in the event of it breaking.

   **The Rig**
   Check that all the ropes are secure and in good condition and that the sail is free from splits or tears. Masts and booms should be checked for signs of wear and replaced if necessary.

   **Essential spares**
   You should consider carrying with you some spare line for your outhaul/downhaul and a means of attracting attention (a Dayglo flag and/or whistle).

   **REMEMBER THE MOST COMMON NEED FOR RESCUE IS EQUIPMENT FAILURE.**

2. **Tell someone where you are going and when you will be back**
   It is recommended that you always windsurf at a location that has safety provision.
   As an extra precaution always ensure that a responsible person knows that you have gone
   out on the water, what time you expect to be back and remember to tell them when you
   have returned.

3. **Obtain a weather forecast for the local sailing area**
   This will prevent you getting caught in changing conditions. If you are sailing at a new
   location it is advisable to seek advice from experienced local windsurfers.

4. **Are you capable of handling the prevailing conditions?**
   Ensure that you are adequately experienced to deal with the conditions that you are going
   out in. Developing your skills in more challenging conditions should take place at a safe
   location which ideally has safety provision.

   **IF IN DOUBT, DON'T GO OUT!**

5. **Windsurf with others**
   It is more fun to windsurf with other people. Not only will you learn from each other but
   also there will be somebody close should you need help.

6. **Avoid strong tides, offshore winds and poor visibility**
   Offshore winds and tidal streams can sweep you away from the safety of your chosen
   sailing area. It is essential that you understand the conditions you are windsurfing in and
   any dangers that may be present. Windsurfing in poor visibility should be avoided because
   you cannot see any dangers or landmarks and it prevents others from seeing you if you get
   into difficulty.

7. **Consider other water-users**
   Many windsurfing locations are used by a variety of other water-users, so always respect
   others on the water by giving them space and take the necessary action to avoid a
   collision. Ensure you have adequate third party insurance, this is free as a benefit to RYA
   Windsurfing Members (see www.rya.org.uk).

## Attracting Attention

However, sometimes conditions or circumstances are simply out of your control and you may need assistance. If this happens there are a variety of simple ways of attracting the attention of an instructor, a safety boat, or the nearest person to you. These people may be able to help you or if not alert others on land who can.

- **The International Distress Signal**
  By repeatedly raising and lowering your arms at either side of your body while kneeling or sitting on your board.

- **Waving a Dayglo flag or similar**
  Either a Dayglo flag (available from www.rya.org.uk), some bright material such as a hat or other piece of clothing can be waved at a source of rescue. This can be incredibly effective even over large distances.

- **Blowing a whistle**
  This is a handy way to attract the attention of people close to you. Provided the wind is not too strong or in the wrong direction, as the sound could simply get carried away.

Take action **IMMEDIATELY** as soon as you realise you need help.

# Self-rescue

There may be times when you need to help yourself and perform a self-rescue, but only consider this when there are no other rescue options. Some of the self-rescue techniques listed below can also be used for getting to and from your sailing area.

### Flagging
If you are struggling to get downwind because you are too tired or the wind is too strong you can use a technique known as **'flagging downwind'**.

- From your secure position, lean the rig towards the front of the board until both board and sail are pointing downwind. As you move the rig remember to counterbalance with your body.

- Stand just behind the rig with your feet either side of the mastfoot and let the wind blow you downwind.

- By leaning the rig to one side or the other you can steer.

**Plus points**
- Possible in any wind strength.
- Quick and easy.

**Minus points**
- Balance is not easy in choppy water.
- Only useful for getting back downwind.

### Butterfly

In no wind, or very light wind conditions when you are unable to sail, you can self-rescue using the **butterfly method.**

- Lay the boom on the back of the board with the mastfoot still attached so that the rig is out of the water. On some models of board you may need to lower your boom height so that it fits on the back of the board.
- Lie at the front of the board with your feet resting on the sail.
- Paddle back to the shore.

**Plus points**
- Very quick and efficient.
- Great over short distances.

**Minus points**
- Difficult to maintain the rig's position in choppy conditions or over long distance.

- Difficult to perform in medium to strong wind conditions.

### Full de-rig

This method is, as the name suggests, an extreme style of self-rescue, requiring you to take apart the rig enabling you to paddle ashore without the rig hindering you. Use of the full de-rig to self-rescue should only be considered as a last resort because de-rigging in open water is extremely difficult.

---

**Top tips**

- **ALWAYS** paddle or steer to the nearest bit of land rather than trying to get back to where you launched.

- **NEVER** abandon the board as it is additional buoyancy.

# An additional method

### Turtle

Another technique to help self-rescue in no wind or very light wind conditions, when it is a struggle to sail, is the **turtle method**.

1. Kneel or sit in the middle of the board facing forwards and detach the rig, pulling it alongside the board with the mastfoot facing forwards and holding onto the mast.

2. Pull the rig over your head with the boom in front of you and lie down with your upper body through the gap between the boom and sail. You are now lying on the inside of the boom with the sail over the top of you. The mastfoot should be facing forwards with the boom clear of water.

**Plus points**
- Can be used over long distances.
- This technique suits all models of boards.

**Minus points**
- slightly tricky to get into the right position.
- Difficult to do in strong winds and choppy conditions, so should only be performed in light winds.

3. Paddle back to the shore.

# CHAPTER 14

# Points of Sailing

The **points of sailing** are the terms given to the course or direction a windsurfer can sail in relation to the wind. Knowing these terms will give you a greater understanding of windsurfing whether participating, observing others or talking about your technique with friends.

The diagram opposite illustrates the different names given to the directions that you can sail in, and those that you can't.

### Sailing Across the Wind
When you are sailing at 90° to the wind you are on a **beam reach**.

The terms 'left' and 'right' are not used in windsurfing to describe direction because it would be confusing once you have turned around to come back the other way. Instead, the terms **port**, **starboard** and **tack** are used. If the wind is blowing onto the left-hand side of your board first and you have your left hand and left foot closest to the front of the board in your sailing position, you are described as being on **port tack**. If the wind is blowing onto the right-hand side of your board first and you have your right hand and right foot forwards, you are sailing on **starboard tack**.

### Sailing Upwind
A board cannot sail directly into the wind. It can, however, sail at an angle of approximately 45° in either direction to the wind. This upwind course is described as **close hauled**.

The area between the two close hauled courses, on either side of the wind direction, is called the **no-go zone**. If you sail too close to the wind into the no-go zone the sail loses all power and you will slow down and stop. When you are sailing upwind you should always be aware of where the wind is coming from so that you stay on the edge of the no-go zone. Having something to aim for (i.e. a new goal point for your close-hauled course) is very helpful, and the more you practise, the quicker you will start to feel when you are getting too close to the wind.

### Sailing Downwind
When heading further away from the wind than a beam reach you are sailing on a **broad reach**. If you sail directly downwind then you are on a **run**.

### Steering and types of turn
As mentioned earlier, to avoid confusion the terms left and right are not used in windsurfing. As a result, when you are steering or turning, different terms are also used.
When steering upwind you **head up** or steer to **windward**.
When steering downwind you **bear away** or steer to **leeward**.
**Tacking** is a turn where you take the nose of the board through the wind.
**Gybing** is a turn where you take the tail of the board through the wind.

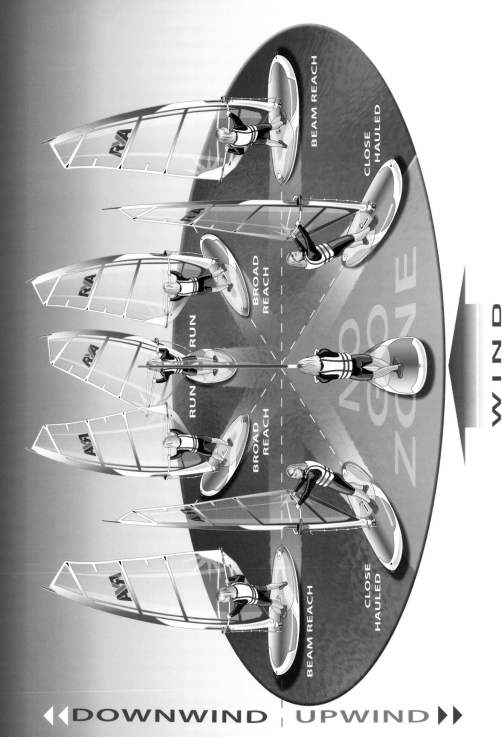

# CHAPTER 15

# Sailing Upwind and Improving Tacking

With the skills learnt so far you can now sail across the wind and steer to avoid obstacles, have more control over the board and you can turn around or tack to get back to where you started.

This next section will introduce you to sailing upwind, a skill which will require practice and help you become more proficient at tacking.

As explained in **'points of sailing'** (page 42), it is not possible to sail directly into the wind. It is however possible to sail very close to the wind on either of the close-hauled directions. Using this knowledge you can sail to a goal point directly upwind by zigzagging on either side of the no-go zone, improving your tacking skills as you change from one close-hauled direction to the other.

**A step-by-step approach to sailing upwind:**

1. While sailing across the wind, pick a new goal point closer to the wind.

   Look at the upwind goal point and steer the front of the board upwind towards the new goal using the techniques you learned in **steering** (page 30).

2. When you are heading towards your new upwind goal point, remember to bring the rig back to the normal sailing position and pull in slightly with your back hand.

   You are now sailing upwind on the edge of the no-go zone on a close-hauled course.

3. Tack the board (remember how you learned earlier on page 32) and start sailing across the wind in the opposite direction.

4. Repeat the process of steering upwind onto a close-hauled sailing course in your new direction.

You are now **zigzagging** around the **no-go zone** making progress upwind.

---

**Top tips for sailing upwind**

- Always have a new upwind goal point to aim for. This helps you to sail upwind and keeps you aware of, and on the edge of, the no-go zone.

- Remember to counter balance the movement of the rig with your body weight whenever steering or tacking.

- When sailing close-hauled remember to keep the sail pulled in slightly with your back hand.

---

HOT TOP TIP

**Flagging**

Having sailed upwind a useful way of getting back downwind is to practise the self-rescue technique of flagging (page 39).

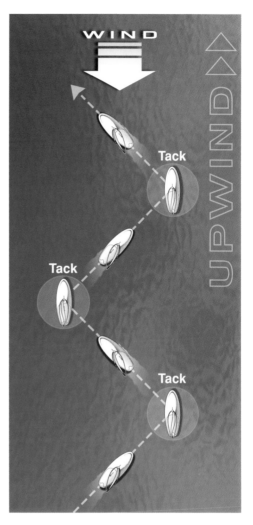

To reach an upwind goal, tack and then sail on a close-hauled course on the edge of the No-Go Zone.

# CHAPTER 16

# Sailing Downwind and Gybing

Now that you can sail upwind and are fine-tuning your tacks it is time to learn to sail downwind and another method of turning around, the **gybe**. This, in combination with everything you have learnt so far, will enable you to sail on any point of sailing in any direction.

## Sailing downwind

Sailing with the wind, or downwind, is as much an integral part of windsurfing as sailing in any other direction. However, when you head downwind you will experience more power in the sail and so must always keep your body lower and remember to use your body more to effectively counter balance the increased pull of the rig.

The direction that you can sail when heading downwind is unrestricted - there is no **no-go zone** as can be seen in the **points of sailing** diagram (page 43). Whether on a **broad reach** or a **run** you will still be able to reach your intended destination downwind.

Generally, however, the easiest and most stable point of sail when learning to sail downwind is a **broad reach**. If you wish to reach a point directly downwind you can zigzag from **broad reach** to **broad reach** using the gybe to change direction.

**Sailing downwind:**

1.  While sailing across the wind select a new goal point further away from the wind and place your back hand slightly further down the boom.

**2.** Using the technique you learned in **steering** (page 30), draw the rig across your body and towards the front of the board extending your front arm and pulling in with your back arm. The board will steer away from the wind. As the rig moves in front of you remember to drop your body back and keep low.

**3.** When heading towards your new downwind goal point, bring the rig back to the normal sailing position and ease out slightly with your back hand.

**You are now sailing downwind.**

## The Gybe

The **Gybe** is a turn used when sailing downwind and occurs when the tail of the board goes through the 'eye' of the wind as the nose passes downwind. You may have experienced this style of turn when practising basic turning by passing the sail over the nose of the board instead of the tail.

Step-by-step approach to a gybe:

1. From your downwind sailing position, continue to steer further away from the wind, using the same technique as before. When the front of the board is pointing directly downwind, ease out with the back hand.

2. **Foot change**
   Move your front foot back down the board over the centreline, in front of your back foot, moving your back foot up to the mastfoot. Your feet will now be in your new sailing position.

3. **Rig change**
   Slide your front hand towards the mast and release your back hand from the boom allowing the rig to swing over the nose of the board. Reach across your body and grab the mast or the other side of the boom, letting go with your other hand.

**4.** Pick a new goal point across the wind and get into the sailing position in the new direction. If zigzagging to a destination downwind then, once the gybe is finished and you are heading back across the wind in the opposite direction, you can steer onto your new downwind course.

You have now turned your board around using a **gybe**.

### Top tips for sailing downwind and gybing

- Remember to always pull in with the back hand when *steering* downwind and to ease out with the back hand when *sailing on a course* downwind.

- Drop your body back and keep low to counter balance the movement and slightly increased power in the rig when heading downwind.

- To control excess power in the rig when heading downwind, move your feet further back down the board and get your body position even lower.

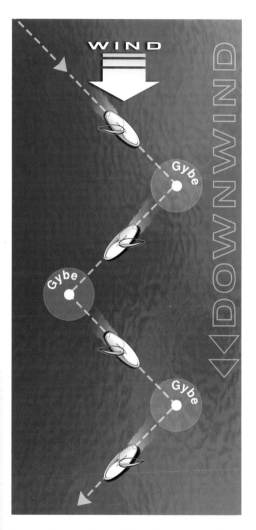

To reach your downwind goal you can sail a course called a run with the wind directly behind you, or zig zag downwind - using a broad reach course and gybing.

# CHAPTER 17

# How a Windsurfer Works

Now that you are windsurfing, this section gives you a brief insight into how it all works, and it will help you consolidate and build on what you have already learned.

### The Sail

While windsurfing you will probably have noticed that the pull, or *drive,* in the sail tends to always come from the same place - about one-third of the way in from the mast and at around head height - as a result you tend to hold the boom in the corresponding place.

This pull, or drive, in the sail is known as the **'centre of effort'**.

### The Board

Although the sail's 'drive' is trying to push the board sideways you still move in a forward direction. This is caused by various parts of the board creating resistance to the sideways force of the sail, namely the daggerboard, the fin and the water-line length of the board (the length of the board actually in contact with the water). With the sail pushing sideways one way and the board pushing back the other way - just like a bar of soap being squeezed between two hands - the board is forced out between these two forces in a forward direction.

The resistance along the length of the board has a central point - just behind the daggerboard - around which the board will turn. This central, or pivot point is known as the **'centre of lateral resistance'**. If you retract the daggerboard while sailing then your pivot point moves back slightly, towards the fin.

### How a board steers

Steering and controlling direction, as you will have learned, is achieved by moving the sail either towards the back of the board to go upwind; towards the front of the board to go downwind; or by keeping the rig upright to go in a straight line. As you adjust the position of your sail you are moving the **centre of effort** (CE) in relation to the pivot point, or **centre of lateral resistance** (CLR).

When the rig is **tilted back**, the centre of effort ends up behind the pivot point, or centre of lateral resistance. The sails 'drive' against the back of the board causing the board to pivot and the nose of the board to turn upwind, enabling us to steer / sail on a course upwind.

When the rig is **tilted forwards**, the exact opposite happens. The 'drive' in the sail pushes against the nose of the board and turns and pivots the board downwind, enabling us to steer / sail on a **course downwind**.

When the rig is **upright**, the CE lies directly above the pivot point, or CLR. The 'drive' in the sail pushes against the CLR itself rather than behind or in front of it and so causes the board to track in a **straight line**.

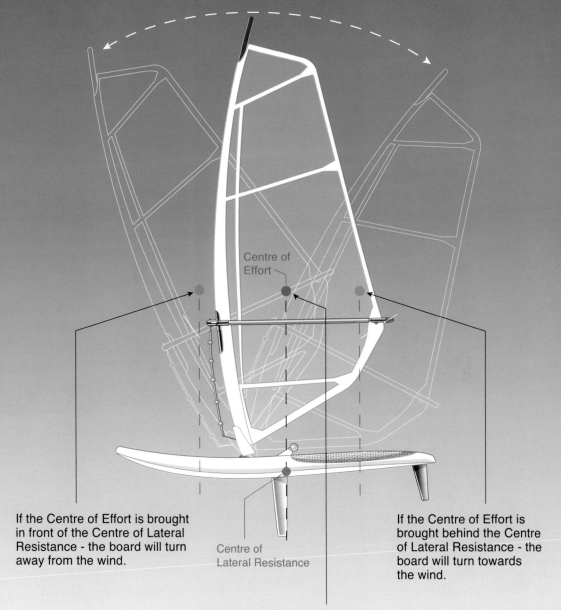

Centre of
Effort

Centre of
Lateral Resistance

If the Centre of Effort is brought in front of the Centre of Lateral Resistance - the board will turn away from the wind.

If the Centre of Effort is brought behind the Centre of Lateral Resistance - the board will turn towards the wind.

With the Centre of Effort and Centre of Lateral Resistance in a line - the board will sail straight.

The illustration shows how moving the Centre of Effort infront and behind the Centre of Lateral Resistance will make the board turn.

# CHAPTER 18

# Avoiding Other Craft

Now you are cruising around on your windsurfer, it is necessary to learn some basic rules of safety and how to be courteous to other water users.

**The most important rule of all is to keep a good lookout at all times.**

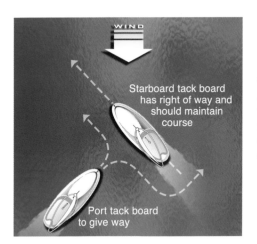

### Port gives way to Starboard
If you are sailing on port tack you should keep out of the way of another board or boat that is sailing in the opposite direction on starboard tack. An easy way to remember this is if your front hand on the boom is your right (or starboard) hand, then you have the right of way over anyone coming in the other direction.

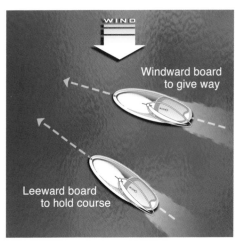

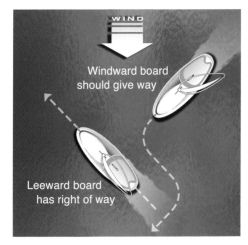

### Windward gives way to Leeward
When two boards are sailing on the same tack, the windward board - the one closest to the source of the wind - must give way to the leeward board, the one furthest downwind.

## Overtaking

When overtaking, the overtaking board must keep clear. In addition, and to avoid confusion, the board ahead must hold its course to allow the overtaking board to pass either side.

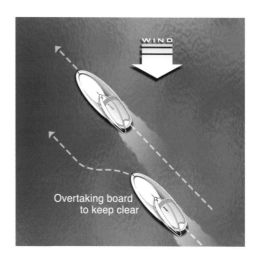

Overtaking board to keep clear

## Other craft

As a general guideline, power should normally give way to sail. However, as a manoeuvrable craft, a windsurfer must stay well clear of any vessel that is restricted in its ability to manoeuvre, such as ferries, fishing boats when they are fishing and supertankers. In general it is advisable to stay out of all shipping channels.

### AVOID COLLISIONS AT ALL COSTS

As an overriding golden rule, you should always try to avoid collisions. In practice, all incidents may be avoided if you are watchful and considerate to other water-users.

# Choosing a Windsurfing Location

Windsurfing is a fantastic sport and can be done almost anywhere provided that there are the two main ingredients - wind and water. While learning the sport, it is important that you have a controlled environment in which you can focus on learning the sport itself rather than worrying about any external factors such as the conditions or your general safety on the water. As a result, it is always advisable to start windsurfing at an RYA Recognised Training Centre.

Once you have mastered the fundamentals of the sport and are sailing around on all points of sailing, tacking and gybing, then you may become interested in trying out a new location.

The safety points covered earlier (page 36) advising on how to windsurf safely and responsibly are essential in helping you to choose when and where you sail. Above all, the **seven common senses** (page 36 'Safety and Self-rescue') provide all the criteria needed to help you choose a good location and have an enjoyable, safe time sailing at a new area.

There are, however, a couple of factors mentioned in the seven common senses which should be expanded upon when considering a windsurfing location. These are based on the main ingredients for the sport - wind and water, or wind and weather, and tides.

## Wind and weather

To go windsurfing you will need wind of a suitable strength and direction, in addition to this air and water temperature is crucial.

This information is available from weather forecasts available from many sources: the internet; television; radio; telephone; fax; newspapers and your local windsurf shop, or RYA Training Centre.

Some forecasts, however, are more relevant to the windsurfer than others and can sometimes appear to be complicated with charts and explanations. The best plan is to collate information from three or four different forecasts in order to get an overall picture for the area where you are going.

Following is a little more detail on the information used in a forecast that can be helpful to you as a windsurfer.

## Wind Strength

Wind speed is measured in **miles per hour**, or knots (nautical miles per hour), for UK shipping forecasts. The ideal wind strength while learning to windsurf and improving your techniques is between 1-6 knots.

As well as units of measurement for wind speed, wind strength is also referred to in terms of **forces** according to the **Beaufort Scale**, ideal wind strength being Force 1-2.

The **Beaufort Scale**, a useful chart to help determine the wind strength:

| Force | Wind speed | Description | Signs on the Land | Sea state |
|---|---|---|---|---|
| 0 | < 1 knot | Calm | Calm, smoke rises vertically. | Sea like a mirror. |
| 1 | 1–3 knots | Light Air | Light flags start to stir and smoke drifts away from vertical. | Ripples with the appearance of scales are formed, but without foam crests. |
| 2 | 4–6 knots | Light Breeze | Wind felt on face; flags start to indicate; leaves start to rustle. | Small wavelets, still short but more pronounced. Crests have a glassy appearance and do not break. An ideal time to learn to windsurf! |
| 3 | 7–10 knots | Gentle Breeze | Leaves and small twigs in constant motion; flags extend but remain below horizontal. | Large wavelets. Crests begin to break, perhaps scattered with horses/foaming tops. |
| 4 | 11–15 knots | Moderate Breeze | Small branches move on trees and flags are fully extended horizontally. Small pieces of paper blow along the ground. | Waves have more frequent white horses/foaming tops. Beginners should head for the shore. |
| 5 | 16–21 knots | Fresh Breeze | The tops of large trees move and small trees sway. Flags may be extended above horizontal. | Moderate waves, taking pronounced long form; many white horses are formed and a chance of spray. |
| 6 | 22-27 knots | Strong Breeze | Wind whistles through telephone lines and large trees sway. Flags blow above horizontal. | Large waves begin to form; the foam crests are more extensive and probably spray. |

## Wind Direction

The direction the wind is blowing in is referred to either in terms of the points of a compass or in relation to the shore that you may be sailing from. When referred to in terms of the points of the compass, the wind direction is where the wind is coming from. For instance, a southerly wind is when the wind is blowing from the south.

Wind direction, when referred to in relation to a shoreline, is best described as **onshore**, **cross-shore** or **offshore**. Combinations of these are also used eg: **cross onshore**.

The best wind direction to sail at this stage as a beginner is either **onshore** or **cross-onshore** as this will always blow you back to the beach if you get into any difficulty.

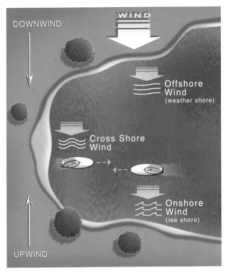

**Wind direction terms**

**Cross-shore** winds can also be good but you should make sure that there is a good area to land directly downwind in case you drift when out on the water.

The one wind direction to avoid is **offshore**. Firstly, because you will have a long walk or swim home if you drift with the wind while windsurfing. Secondly with an offshore breeze the wind strength may seem light and the water may look calm next to the shore, but further out on the water the wind will be a lot stronger and the water will get progressively rougher - not good conditions for you to improve your windsurfing skills.

## Temperature

As highlighted in the 'seven common senses' (page 36) you should always check that you have the correct personal equipment for the conditions - a wetsuit and buoyancy aid etc. - before going out sailing. Knowing in advance by checking the forecast, how warm or cold the air and water temperature will be helps you to choose the right equipment to take and makes your windsurfing session more comfortable and enjoyable.

## Sun or Rain

Sunny, clear days can provide the most pleasant conditions out on the water, but to avoid restricting your sailing time too much throughout the year you should consider heading out on cloudy days as well! However heavy rain, hail and snow conditions should be avoided.

# Tides

Tides are the horizontal and vertical movement of the earth's seas and oceans, they are the reason moored boats point in the same direction in a harbour when there is no wind and why debris and seaweed are strewn neatly in a line at the top of a beach even though the water is a long way further back down the beach.

If you are sailing on inland waters, for example a lake or reservoir, then tide will not be a factor in your windsurfing. But if you are considering windsurfing at a tidal location such as a harbour or protected bay, then you must be aware of important factors such as when to go out windsurfing and how the venue may differ at different states of the tide. With this information you will be able to windsurf safely and to maximise your enjoyment while out on the water.

## When to go windsurfing

Daily tide times giving details of when the tide is in, otherwise known as a **high tide**, and when it is out, known as a **low tide**, are available from many different sources; newspapers, the internet, radio, television, fax and telephone. One of the most common sources for tide times are **tide tables** that are available in local harbour offices, windsurfing, sailing, diving and surfing shops.

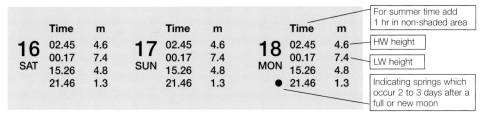

An extract from a tide table showing day, date, high water, low water and tidal height.

Because the movement of water, or the tidal stream, is usually at its strongest midway between high and low tide you may choose to go sailing at or around high or low water, depending on the location.

## Sailing venues and different states of tide

It is a good idea to get a view of your chosen venue at different states of the tide to familiarise yourself with factors such as a tricky launching and landing area at high tide or perhaps a long walk back up the beach at low tide.

You should also speak with other water-users at the location to learn other useful information such as the positions of obstacles like rocks that may be submerged or hidden at certain states of the tide. As your windsurfing improves at different locations, so will your ability to successfully judge the suitability of a particular location to your capability.

Now you have tried one of the most diverse and exciting sports it's time to develop your skills and perhaps look to windsurf in slightly stronger winds. If you are not already addicted 'what comes next' is where the fun and excitement really gets you hooked.

Following, are a few pages explaining how to progress from completing your initial introduction to the sport during a start windsurfing course to the skills taught and developed on the intermediate course.

Most importantly, have fun and see you on the water!

*Amanda*

**Amanda Van Santen**
**Chief Windsurfing Instructor**

# CHAPTER 20

# What's Next

Once you have completed the Start Windsurfing Course, you will be ready to take the next exciting and exhilarating step towards improving your windsurfing.

The Intermediate Course teaches you how to sail in stronger winds and how to get to grips with the harness, footstraps and more dynamic skills. Additional fun elements for example feasible freestyle may be incorporated to aid board and rig control. Beachstarting and gybing are taught either as a clinic or combined in a course tailored to an individual's needs and the teaching environment.

This course is split into two competencies to encourage smooth progression. At many RYA centres the course will be combined, as the core skills are transferable. Ability and weather conditions will have relevance as to the level achieved.

The incredibly effective and memorable coaching system Fast*fwd*, developed with Simon Bornhoft, is used within the RYA National Windsurfing Scheme to focus on, and enhance, your progression throughout all aspects of the sport from the Intermediate Course upwards.

### A quick insight into Fast*fwd*
Fast*fwd* is an on-water coaching guide and self-reminder system that can become a common language between instructor and student.

Whilst you might concentrate on one particular point at a time, the formula works in a continuous circle and acts as a constant student and instructor prompt. Starting with vision, you'll regularly run through the formula, until you home in on one particular element to sort out a problem, or emphasise a point.

The formula is made up of 5 key elements that form the basis of our actions on a board.

## Vision . Trim . (Counter) Balance . Power . Stance

### "VISION maintains our sailing line"

Where you look, your sailing line and how you use your head, are always the first considerations before any other action. Such a simple point, but it is unquestionably the most important aspect of improving technique.

### "TRIM keeps the board flat"

A flat, stable platform increases the ease with which we can control the board and rig in any situation. All our actions and the other elements in the formula (except **vision**) refer and relate to **trim**.

### "BALANCE forms our framework"

**Balance and counter-balance** refers to our continuous objective of maintaining our distance from the rig (by extending the front arm) and always opposing and **counter-balancing** the rigs pull, and position with our body.

### "POWER channels the rig's forces"

**Power** refers to channeling the rig's forces, by pulling the boom in, back and down, particularly in planing conditions and it is critical in many skills learnt in windsurfing.

### "STANCE is how we use our body"

**Stance** refers to how we position and angle our body in order to control the rig. Some very specific actions can create a range of movement that maximises the effect of our body in a windsurfing environment.

# A Windsurfer's Glossary

### Board:

| | |
|---|---|
| **Nose** | Front of the board. |
| **Tail** | Back of the board. |
| **Deck** | Top of the board. |
| **Hull** | Bottom of the board. |
| **Daggerboard** | Large flat retractable plate providing the board with sideways resistance. |
| **Fin** | Small flat plate attached to the underside and tail of the board providing directional stability, shaped like a dorsal fin. |
| **Mast Track** | A recess on the top of the board to attach the rig. |
| **Centreline** | Imaginary line going through the centre of the board from nose to tail. |
| **Towing Eye** | A small hole in the nose of the board used to attached a rope to enable towing. |

### Rig:

| | |
|---|---|
| **Mast** | Long tapered pole used to hold the sail up. |
| **Sail** | The 'engine' of the windsurfer - delivering power to the windsurfer. |
| **Battens** | Stiff, flexible rods providing strength and shape to a sail. |
| **Boom** | The 'handlebars' of a windsurfer. |
| **Mastfoot** | An attachment joining the board and rig together. |
| **Mast Extension** | An adjustable version of a mastfoot. |
| **Uphaul** | Combined rope and elastic attached to the boom enabling the rig to be pulled out of the water. |
| **Outhaul** | A rope used to attach the clew of the sail to the end of the boom. |
| **Downhaul** | A rope used to attach the tack of the sail to the mastfoot. |

### Clothing:

| | |
|---|---|
| **Wetsuit** | Neoprene suit to keep the body protected and warm. |
| **Buoyancy Aid** | A foam-filled jacket to provide positive buoyancy when immersed. A good buoyancy aid should comply with the CE50 Newton Standard. |
| **Rash Vest** | A T-shirt like garment worn either on its own or under a wetsuit to provide protection. |
| **Booties** | Shoes designed especially for water activities. |

**Background Theory:**

| | |
|---|---|
| **Secure Position** | A stationary positioning of the board where the sail has no power and the board is directly across the wind. |
| **Balance Point** | The point where the sail is drawn across the board and feels light. |
| **Counter Balance** | To oppose the weight of the rig with our body - rig goes one way, body the other. |
| **Goal Point** | A point chosen to aim for when sailing. |
| **Sailing Position** | The position we adopt to go windsurfing. |
| **To Tack** | A turn that takes the nose of the board through the wind. |
| **To Gybe** | A turn that takes the nose of the board away from the wind. |
| **Upwind** | In a position closer to the wind than you. |
| **Downwind** | In a position further away from the wind then you are. |
| **Across Wind** | At 90° to the wind direction. |
| **Close Hauled** | A direction approximately 45° away from the direction of the wind. |
| **Beam Reach** | A direction approximately 90° away from the direction of the wind. |
| **Broad Reach** | A direction approximately 135° away from the direction of the wind. |
| **Run** | A direction approximately 180° away from the direction of the wind. |
| **No-Go Zone** | An area approximately 45° either side of the wind direction into which it is not possible to sail or windsurf. |
| **Head Up** | To steer the board closer to where the wind is coming from. |
| **Bear Away** | To steer the board away from where the wind is coming from. |
| **Windward** | A place or side of a board/craft that is closer to the wind. |
| **Leeward** | A place or side of a board/craft that is away or sheltered from the wind. |
| **Onshore** | When the wind direction blows directly on to the shore/land. |
| **Offshore** | When the wind direction blows directly off the shore/land. |
| **Cross-shore** | When the wind direction blows directly across the shore/land. |
| **Port** | A nautical term - the direction to the left of somebody facing the front of a board/craft. |
| **Starboard** | A nautical term - the direction to the right of somebody facing the front of a board/craft. |
| **Centre of Effort** | A central point on the sail from where the drive comes from. |

| | |
|---|---|
| **Centre of Lateral Resistance** | A combination of the fin, daggerboard and wetted area of the board that creates directional stability and resists sideways movement. |
| **Port Tack** | A nautical term used to describe the direction to which we are sailing - left side of our body is furthest forward on the board/craft. |
| **Starboard Tack** | A nautical term used to describe the direction to which we are sailing - right side of the body is furthest forward on the board/craft. |
| **Horizontal Tide** | The parallel or sideways motion of the tide along the coastline. |
| **Vertical Tide** | The effect of tidal rise or fall on the land. |
| **Fast*fwd*** | The coaching model used within the National Windsurfing Scheme; vision, trim, balance, power and stance. |

**Measurements of wind speed:**

| | |
|---|---|
| **Miles per hour** | A measurement of speed. |
| **Knots** | Nautical miles per hour. |
| **Beaufort Scale** | An international scale of wind speed described in numerical forces from 0 (calm) to 12 (a hurricane). |

**Forms of rescue:**

| | |
|---|---|
| **Butterfly Rescue** | A form of rescue where the sail is laid on the back of the board and the sailor paddles. |
| **Turtle Rescue** | A form of rescue where the sailor detaches the sail, lays it on the board, climbs inside it and paddles. |
| **Flagging** | A downwind rescue, the sailor, board and rig drift with the wind. |

# Index

# RYA Windsurfing

Log your progression with the **National Windsurfing Scheme Logbook and Syllabus (G47)**

Designed as a logbook suitable for beginner, intermediate and advanced windsurfers, this book also contains essential information on the new and improved RYA Windsurfing Syllabus. It clearly explains how to choose the right course, outlines the content of the syllabus and states the assessment criteria that will be used. RYA National Windsurfing Scheme Logbook and Syllabus also includes a personal log, on which to chart progress, notes pages and space for readers to attach their certificates.

### RYA Intermediate Windsurfing (G51)

RYA Intermediate Windsurfing builds on the manoeuvres learnt in Start Windsurfing. It covers the effective and memorable coaching system, how to get to grips with the harness and footstraps, beachstarting, equipment, and developing tacks and gybes ready for a little more wind.

Written by Simon Bornhoft and edited by Amanda Van Santen.

### RYA Advanced Windsurfing (G52)

Blasting control, waterstarting, tacking, gybing, bump and jump, and advanced carving skills are developed from the intermediate course, continuing the use of coaching and enhancing theoretical knowledge. Each skill, transition or piece of information is explained step by step and combined with photographs or illustrations.

Written by Simon Bornhoft and edited by Amanda Van Santen.

The RYA provides courses encouraging and helping people to become qualified Instructors. Following the same levels as the National Scheme, each instructor course is taught by highly qualified and trained coaches at RYA Training Centres. If you want to pass on your skills and encourages others into the sport of windsurfing, course dates are available on the RYA website **www.rya.org.uk** or by calling RYA Training on **02380 604 181**. All pre and post instructor course information for all levels is also covered in the W33 Instructor Handbook.

**All RYA publications are available online from the RYA Webshop www.rya.org.uk or via the RYA Despatch department on: 0845 345 0372**

# RYA Membership

## Promoting and Protecting Boating
### www.rya.org.uk

# RYA Membership

## Promoting and Protecting Boating

The RYA is the national organisation which represents the interests of everyone who goes boating for pleasure.

The greater the membership, the louder our voice when it comes to protecting members' interests.

Apply for membership today, and support the RYA, to help the RYA support you.

### Benefits of Membership

- Access to expert advice on all aspects of boating from legal wrangles to training matters
- Special members' discounts on a range of products and services including boat insurance, books, videos and class certificates
- Free issue of certificates of competence, increasingly asked for by everyone from overseas governments to holiday companies, insurance underwriters to boat hirers

- Access to the wide range of RYA publications, including the quarterly magazine
- Third Party insurance for windsurfing members
- Free Internet access with RYA-Online
- Special discounts on AA membership
- Regular offers in RYA Magazine
- ...and much more

**Join now - membership form opposite**

### Join online at *www.rya.org.uk*

Visit our website for information, advice, members' services and web shop.

**1** **Important** To help us comply with Data Protection legislation, please tick *either* Box A or Box B (you must tick Box A to ensure you receive the full benefits of RYA membership). The RYA will not pass your data to third parties.

☐ **A.** I wish to join the RYA and receive future information on member services, benefits (as listed in RYA Magazine and website) and offers.

☐ **B.** I wish to join the RYA but do not wish to receive future information on member services, benefits (as listed in RYA Magazine and website) and offers.

## When completed, please send this form to: RYA, RYA House, Ensign Way, Hamble, Southampton, SO31 4YA

**2**

| | Title | Forename | Surname | Date of Birth | Male | Female |
|---|---|---|---|---|---|---|
| **1.** | | | | DD / MM / YY | ☐ | ☐ |
| **2.** | | | | DD / MM / YY | ☐ | ☐ |
| **3.** | | | | DD / MM / YY | ☐ | ☐ |
| **4.** | | | | DD / MM / YY | ☐ | ☐ |

Address

Town                County                Post Code

Evening Telephone                Daytime Telephone

email

Signature:                Date:

**3** **Type of membership required:** *(Tick Box)*

☐ **Personal** Annual rate £37 or £34 by Direct Debit
From 1st October 2007 annual rate £39 or £36 by Direct Debit

☐ **Under 21** Annual rate £12 (no reduction for Direct Debit)
From 1st October 2007 annual rate £13

☐ **Family\*** Annual rate £56 or £52 by Direct Debit
From 1st October 2007 annual rate £58 or £54 by Direct Debit

*\* Family Membership: 2 adults plus any under 21s all living at the same address*

**4** Please tick ONE box to show your main boating interest.

☐ Yacht Racing        ☐ Yacht Cruising
☐ Dinghy Racing       ☐ Dinghy Cruising
☐ Personal Watercraft ☐ Inland Waterways
☐ Powerboat Racing    ☐ Windsurfing
☐ Motor Boating       ☐ Sportsboats and RIBs

Please see Direct Debit form overleaf

# RYA

## Instructions to your Bank or Building Society to pay by Direct Debit

Please complete this form and return it to:
Royal Yachting Association, RYA House, Ensign Way, Hamble, Southampton, Hampshire SO31 4YA

**DIRECT Debit**

To The Manager: _____ Bank/Building Society

Address: _____

Post Code: _____

**Originators Identification Number**

| 9 | 5 | 5 | 2 | 1 | 3 |
|---|---|---|---|---|---|

**5. RYA Membership Number (For office use only)**

_____

**2. Name(s) of account holder(s)**

_____

_____

**6. Instruction to pay your Bank or Building Society**

Please pay Royal Yachting Association Direct Debits from the account detailed in this instruction subject to the safeguards assured by The Direct Debit Guarantee.
I understand that this instruction may remain with the Royal Yachting Association and, if so, details will be passed electronically to my Bank/Building Society.

**3. Branch Sort Code**

| | — | | — | |
|---|---|---|---|---|

**4. Bank or Building Society account number**

| | | | | | | |
|---|---|---|---|---|---|---|

Signature(s) _____

Date _____

Banks and Building Societies may not accept Direct Debit instructions for some types of account

**Cash, Cheque, Postal Order enclosed** £ _____

Made payable to the Royal Yachting Association

**Office use / Centre Stamp**

| **077** | **Office use only:** Membership Number Allocated _____ |
|---|---|